ROOTS AND BLUES MANDOLIN

By Steve James

Publisher: David A. Lusterman
Group Publisher and Editorial Director: Dan Gabel
Editor: Jeffrey Pepper Rodgers
Music Editor and Engraver: Andrew DuBrock
Art Director: Barbara Summer
Photographs: Unless otherwise noted, all photos by George Brainard

© 2010 Steve James
ISBN 978-1-890490-79-9

This book was produced by Stringletter, Inc.
PO Box 767, San Anselmo, CA 94979-0767
(415) 485-6946; Stringletter.com

Library of Congress Cataloging-in-Publication Data

James, Steve, 1950-
  Roots and blues mandolin / by Steve James.
    p. cm. — (Acoustic guitar private lessons)
  Includes bibliographical references and index.
  ISBN 978-1-890490-79-9 (alk. paper)
  1. Mandolin–Methods (Blues)–Self-instruction. 2. Blues (Music)–Instruction and study. I. Title.
  MT608.J36 2010
  787.8'41931643–dc22
                        2010017527

Contents

The complete set of audio tracks for the musical examples and songs in *Roots and Blues Mandolin* is available for free download at AcousticGuitar.com/RBMAudio. Just add the tracks to your shopping cart and enter the discount code "RBMTracks12" during checkout to activate your free download.

Introduction

"I didn't know you could play blues on a mandolin!"

Those of us who do play blues mandolin hear that comment frequently from people who associate the instrument with other musical forms. Of course, you can play just about anything on a mandolin; its unmistakable voice has been heard from the earliest incarnations of blues up to the contemporary roots music revival. Only recently, however, has any instructional material become available for blues mandolin. The positive response to my DVD lessons for Homespun, along with Rich Delgrosso's book (*Mandolin Blues*) on the styles of early blues mandolin masters, indicated that more on the subject would be welcome—especially about the basics of style and song that are presented here.

This volume is both a songbook and a playing method. There are no exercises or practice regimens, but the tunes and accompaniments contain essential mandolin playing techniques, some generally useful rhythm and harmony ideas, and licks and phrases basic to the blues vocabulary. These are pointed up largely in the context of the pieces in which they are used. The sequence is geared toward players who already know some blues on another instrument, such as guitar, and would like to double on mandolin, or to those with some mandolin experience who want to add blues songs and sounds to their repertoire.

I hope *Roots and Blues Mandolin* will also encourage some blues lovers who have never played, but often wished they could, to take up this versatile and welcoming little instrument and give a voice to the music they've always heard and felt.

There's all kinds of trouble you can't get into when you're playing a mandolin. Please do.

Steve James
Austin, Texas

TRACK 1 **Introduction**

Music Notation Key

The music in this book is written in standard notation and tablature. Here's how to read it.

STANDARD NOTATION

Standard notation is written on a five-line staff. Notes are written in alphabetical order from A to G.

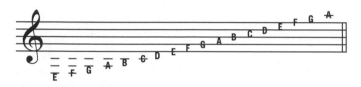

The duration of a note is determined by three things: the note head, stem, and flag. A whole note (𝅝) equals four beats. A half note (𝅗𝅥) is half of that: two beats. A quarter note (𝅘𝅥) equals one beat, an eighth note (𝅘𝅥𝅮) equals half of one beat, and a 16th note (𝅘𝅥𝅯) is a quarter beat (there are four 16th notes per beat).

The fraction (4/4, 3/4, 6/8, etc.) or ¢ character shown at the beginning of a piece of music denotes the time signature. The top number tells you how many beats are in each measure, and the bottom number indicates the rhythmic value of each beat (4 equals a quarter note, 8 equals an eighth note, 16 equals a 16th note, and 2 equals a half note). The most common time signature is 4/4, which signifies four quarter notes per measure and is sometimes designated with the symbol ¢ (for common time). The symbol ¢ stands for cut time (2/2). Most songs are either in 4/4 or 3/4.

TABLATURE

In tablature, the four horizontal lines represent the four string pairs of the mandolin, with the first string on the top and fourth on the bottom. The numbers refer to fret numbers on a given string. The notation and tablature in this book are designed to be used in tandem—refer to the notation to get the rhythmic information and note durations, and refer to the tablature to get the exact locations of the notes on the mandolin fingerboard.

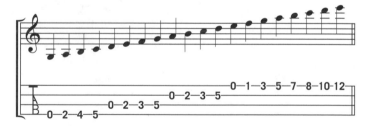

FINGERINGS AND PICK DIRECTIONS

Fingerings are indicated with small numbers and letters in the notation. Fretting-hand fingering is indicated with 1 for the index finger, 2 the middle, 3 the ring, 4 the pinky, and *T* the thumb.

In music played with a flatpick, downstrokes (toward the floor) and upstrokes (toward the ceiling) are shown as follows. Slashes in the notation indicate a strum through the previously played chord. Tremolo (fast down- and upstrokes with the pick) is shown with the symbol below.

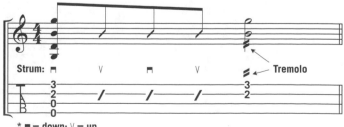

CHORD DIAGRAMS

Chord diagrams show where the fingers go on the fingerboard. Frets are shown horizontally. The thick top line represents the nut. A fret number to the right of a diagram indicates a chord played higher up the neck (in this case the top horizontal line is thin). Strings are shown as vertical lines. The line on the far left represents the fourth (lowest) string, and the line on the far right represents the first (highest) string. Dots show where the fingers go, and thick horizontal lines indicate barres. Numbers above the diagram are left-hand finger numbers, as used in standard notation. Again, the fingerings are only suggestions. An *X* indicates a string that should be muted or not played; 0 indicates an open string.

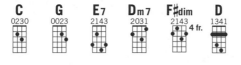

TUNINGS

Alternate mandolin tunings are given from the lowest (fourth) string to the highest (first) string. For instance, G D A D indicates standard tuning with the highest string dropped to D. Standard notation for songs in alternate tunings always reflects the actual pitches of the notes. Arrows underneath tuning notes indicate strings that are altered from standard tuning and whether they are tuned up or down.

ARTICULATIONS

There are a number of ways you can articulate a note on the mandolin. Notes connected with slurs (not to be confused with ties) in the tablature or standard notation are articulated with either a hammer-on, pull-off, or slide. Lower notes slurred to higher notes are played as hammer-ons; higher notes slurred to lower notes are played as pull-offs. While it's usually obvious that slurred notes are played as hammer-ons or pull-offs, an *H* or *P* is included above the tablature as an extra reminder.

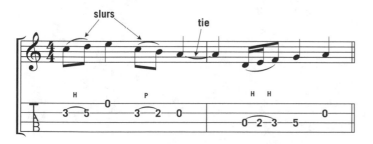

Slides are represented with a dash, and an *S* is included above the tab. A dash preceding a note represents a slide into the note from an indefinite point in the direction of the slide; a dash following a note indicates a slide off of the note to an indefinite point in the direction of the slide. For two slurred notes connected with a slide, you should pick the first note and then slide into the second.

Grace notes are represented by small notes with a dash through the stem in standard notation and with small numbers in the tab. A grace note is a very quick ornament leading into a note, most commonly executed as a hammer-on, pull-off, or slide. In the first example below, pluck the note at the fifth fret on the beat, then quickly hammer onto the seventh fret. The second example is executed as a quick pull-off from the second fret to the open string. In the third example, both notes at the fifth fret are played simultaneously (even though it appears that the fifth fret, fourth string, is to be played by itself), then the seventh fret, fourth string, is quickly hammered.

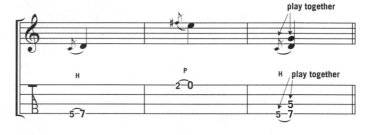

REPEATS

One of the most confusing parts of a musical score can be the navigation symbols, such as repeats, *D.S. al Coda*, *D.C. al Fine*, *To Coda*, etc. Repeat symbols are placed at the beginning and end of the passage to be repeated.

You should ignore repeat symbols with the dots on the right side the first time you encounter them; when you come to a repeat symbol with dots on the left side, jump back to the previous repeat symbol facing the opposite direction (if there is no previous symbol, go to the beginning of the piece). The next time you come to the repeat symbol, ignore it and keep going unless it includes instructions such as "Repeat three times."

A section will often have a different ending after each repeat. The example below includes a first and a second ending. Play until you hit the repeat symbol, jump back to the previous repeat symbol and play until you reach the bracketed first ending, skip the measures under the bracket and jump immediately to the second ending, and then continue.

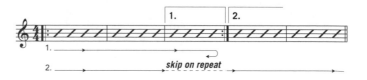

Mandolin was a central voice in string bands like this one, photographed circa 1930. *Mark Weakley Collection.*

The Beginnings of Blues Mandolin

The earliest recordings of blues mandolin date to early 1924, when ruling "race" diva Clara Smith was joined in the studio by mandolinist Clarence Conaway, and blues queen Ma Rainey teamed up with Miles Pruitt. Both men were part of mandolin and guitar playing brother acts; their inclusion on these sessions was part of a new trend toward the incorporation of the string-dominated roots style on popular blues records. The story of blues mandolin, however, starts much earlier.

At the turn of the 20th century, America had gone mandolin mad. Stage acts like the Spanish Figaro Students (who were neither Spanish nor students) that featured the instrument had packed houses since the 1880s. Mandolins manufactured by Lyon and Healy or Gibson augmented the gaiety of the '90s, and the flat-back models they produced began to supplant the older Neapolitan, lute-inspired bowl-back design. By the early 1900s, stage professionals and a legion of amateur clubs and orchestras employed a menagerie of mandolin hybrids in a repertoire that ranged from waltzes, polkas, marches, mazurkas, and reels to the new syncopated music of the ragtime era.

The ascendance of the syncopated string ensemble reached a zenith of sorts in 1912 when the Clef Club Orchestra, under the direction of composer James Reese Europe, became the first African-American group to play Carnegie Hall. At the time, the orchestra's 145 pieces included 47 mandolins! Band member James Weldon Johnson would recall, "New York had not yet become accustomed to jazz, so when the Clef Club opened with a syncopated march . . . the applause became a tumult."

Well before the Clef Club's Carnegie debut, a different brand of syncopated mandolin music was being played from New York to New Orleans. In the Crescent City, for instance, string bands were ubiquitous from street corner to salon. In their varied song bag were the themes, tonality, and rhythm of early jazz and blues. Years before he published his famous "Memphis Blues" (also in 1912), W.C. Handy heard a mandolin-led string trio playing the "new music" during an intermission of his society dance orchestra in Mississippi. The audience, he noted, threw money at them.

By the time blues mandolin was first recorded, it was an established genre. Early waxings by Conaway and Pruitt were soon followed by discs that featured the virtuosity of Texan string wizard Coley Jones, the versatility of Mississippi mandolin master Charlie McCoy, and the force-of-nature pick work of Tennessee powerhouse Yank Rachell . . . to name a few of many. While McCoy and Rachell were busy in Chicago, laying the groundwork for that city's modern blues style, the sound of a hot mandolin was also heard in other kinds of American roots music.

In the 1930s, singing sibling duos were common in popular country music, and among the most prolific were the Monroe Brothers, Charlie and Bill. The latter had honed his prodigious mandolin chops partly under the influence of black Kentucky fiddler Arnold Schultz, and his rapid-fire riffing—shot through with blue notes and phrasing, even on ballads and gospel songs—soon became a key part of the high-octane acoustic string band music that Bill Monroe would call bluegrass.

Meanwhile, in 1937, 21-year-old fiddle hotshot Cliff Bruner entered a San Antonio studio with his now-fabled Texas Wanderers, a septet of young western swing dance-band veterans who could handle waltzes, heart songs, and hoedowns but preferred stomping jazz and blues. In the Wanderer's combustible front line was pioneer electric mandolinist

In the Crescent City, string bands were ubiquitous from street corner to salon. In their varied song bag were the themes, tonality, and rhythm of early jazz and blues.

Pickers in Kendall County, Texas, circa 1983.
James Edward Dreiss/Laura Long Collection/Institute of Texas Cultures.

Leo Raley, who liked to boot his custom-cobbled rig into overdrive and shred as though he were leading a horn section. Raley made the way straight for players like Tiny Moore and Johnny Gimble who would craft the sound through the '40s and '50s and beyond.

While mandolin was heard in bluegrass and western swing, the instrument took a backseat in the amplified blues of the postwar era. T-Bone Walker and Muddy Waters, who had played string band blues as young men in Texas and Mississippi, had left the older styles behind when they cracked the R&B record charts up north and out west. Even senior inventor Rachell favored electric guitar over the instrument whose sound he had redefined a couple of decades earlier.

The situation improved in a way as country blues became part of the pop-folk phenomenon of the 1960s. "Rediscovered" veterans took their music to campuses, coffeehouses, and festival stages where it was heard, and imitated, by an assortment of collegians, collectors, bohemians, and recovering hoootenanophiles. In the early '60s Yank Rachell was reunited with his old playing and recording partner Sleepy John Estes. Soon after, Carl Martin, Ted Bogan, and Howard Armstrong, who had collaborated more than a generation earlier under such sobriquets as the Tennessee Chocolate Drops, returned to studio and stage where they deftly swapped mandolin, fiddle, and guitar as though running some kind of musical broken pass play. Armstrong in particular took his touted musical and verbal eloquence to workshops and music camps where he inspired a platoon of younger players (this writer included).

These circumstances, along with original music coming from sources as disparate as folk/roots fusionist Ry Cooder and Irish pub-rocker Rory Gallagher, plus new discs from under-the-radar stalwarts like Chicagoan Johnny Young, signaled the beginning of a grassroots blues mandolin revival that is still in progress. But that's enough of blues mandolin history for now. If you've read this far, you're already part of it. Let's play.

Tuning and Basic Techniques

The mandolin is a fretted instrument, like the guitar, with four pairs (courses) of metal strings. Each pair is tuned in unison, and adjacent courses are tuned in intervals of a fifth like the violin, which the mandolin resembles in size. From the lowest pitched strings to the highest, the notes are GG DD AA EE.

The strings are attached to a tailpiece at the lower end of the instrument and to eight geared tuning machines at the headstock. They pass over a wooden bridge on the face and a nut at the top of the fingerboard. Proper placement and adjustment of these parts is essential to the playability of the instrument. The mandolin is small and light enough to be held in playing position with the left (fretting) hand and right arm, but is usually supported with a shoulder strap.

Mandolins are made in a wide variety of body styles, any of which are suitable for playing the material presented in this book. Some custom or vintage instruments are quite expensive, but lower priced models work well if properly set up and maintained.

headstock

tuning machines

nut

bridge

tailpiece

Gibson A-40, circa 1942.

Three Harmony-made mandolins: from left to right, circa 1950 Stella, late '30s Strad-o-lin, and circa 1960 Stella.

Vega/Fairbanks banjo mandolin, circa 1917 Gibson F-2, and a contemporary National Reso-Phonic RM custom.

TUNE-UP

Using a pitch reference, electronic tuner, or the tuning track in your *Roots and Blues Mandolin* audio files, tune one of the fourth (lowest pitched) strings to a G below middle C—the same pitch as the third string of a guitar in standard tuning. Tune the second string in the pair in unison with the first. Tune adjacent courses in the same way, in a series of intervals of a fifth. Once the mandolin's four courses are tuned to GG DD AA EE, it's advisable to correct the tuning by repeating this process. Note that an open string creates the same pitch as the string below it played at the seventh fret.

TRACK 2 **Standard Tuning**

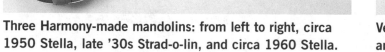

It is worth noting that many blues players have tuned the G and D courses in octaves instead of in unison, substituting an A (second) string for one of the G (fourth) strings and an E (first) string for one of the D (third) strings. With this string setup, you can tune to: gG dD AA EE. The lowercase *g* and *d* indicates that these strings are an octave higher.

USING A PICK

Select a standard-sized, guitar-type pick of medium to heavy thickness. Avoid light, flexible picks; they produce a thin, weak tone and make rapid up- and downstrokes and smooth tremolo more difficult. Flex the fingers of your picking hand inward to make a loose fist (not touching the palm). Place the pick, point outward, on the first joint of your index finger and hold it in place with the ball of your thumb. Put your picking hand over the strings with your wrist slightly arched and you should be in good playing position with the point of the pick perpendicular to the strings. Maintain a relaxed but firm grip and play down- and upstrokes with a rotating wrist motion. Use a little elbow movement for harder strokes, but try to avoid touching the face of the mandolin. The pieces in this book start with a picking pattern that employs only downstrokes and then progress quickly to the use of alternating down- and upstrokes and pick tremolo, explained in further detail where they occur.

FRETTING

Place your fretting hand around the neck and fingerboard of the mandolin so that the inside of the first joint of your index (first) finger lightly touches the treble edge of the fingerboard at the first fret and the ball of your extended thumb rests on the back of the neck on the bass side. Curve your middle (second), ring (third) and little (fourth) fingers over the fingerboard, flexed at each joint so the tips rest on or near the strings. The grip, although more relaxed, is similar to one you would use when hefting a hammer or golf club. Your fretting hand is now in place to play in the first position.

The first finger should be able to access the first and second frets. The middle finger should be able to cover the third and fourth frets; the third should be able to cover the fourth through sixth frets. Rotate your grip to fret lower strings. Avoid the common habit of curling the fourth or little finger against your palm. Keep it over the fingerboard, slightly flexed, just like its larger mates. You're going to need it.

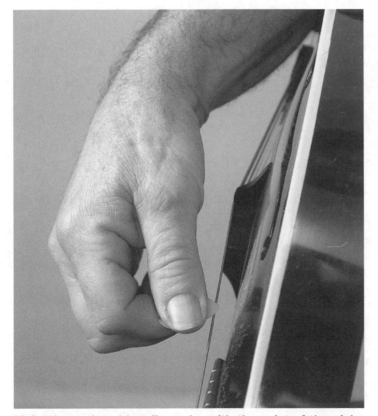

Maintain a relaxed but firm grip, with the point of the pick perpendicular to the strings.

The fretting hand in first position.

SLURS AND MUTING

As with guitar, on a mandolin you will make frequent use of slurs such as slides, pull-offs, and hammer-ons. To play a slide, you fret and pick a note and move the fretting finger up (or down) the fingerboard, usually one fret, to alter the pitch. For a pull-off, you play a note and remove the fretting finger with a downward motion that causes a lower note on the same string to sound. A hammer-on works the opposite way; fret and pick a note with one finger and place an adjacent finger on a higher fret on the same string with enough force to make it sound.

Muting with your fretting hand involves playing a note or chord and then relaxing your grip enough to stop its resonance—an especially effective device when playing rhythm figures to cut down on the mandolin's characteristic jangle.

All of these techniques will be detailed further in the pieces in which they are used.

Blue Notes and Tremolo

The sound of blues music is based in part by the use of three scale intervals: the altered or slurred third, the flatted fifth, and the flatted or dominant seventh. They're not hard to find. Let's start a little lesson in lickology by playing two octaves of a G major scale in the first position using fretted and open strings, and then add the "blue" notes.

Play this sequence slowly at first using all pick downstrokes (**Example 1**). Fret notes at the second fret with your index finger, the third and fourth frets with your middle finger, and the fourth and fifth frets with your ring finger. Even though it's not being used, don't forget to keep your fourth finger in playing position. This position of your fretting hand will be used in most of the pieces in this book.

When you are comfortable playing this scale pattern—open G string to E string at the third fret—try playing it a faster tempo with alternating down- and upstrokes of the pick, from the lowest note to highest and then from highest to lowest (**Example 2**).

Now add the blue notes: the flatted third (B♭), the flatted fifth (D♭), and the flatted or

TRACK 3 **Ex. 1: G-major scale (played with all downstrokes)**

TRACK 4 **Ex. 2: G-major scale (played with alternating down- and upstrokes)**

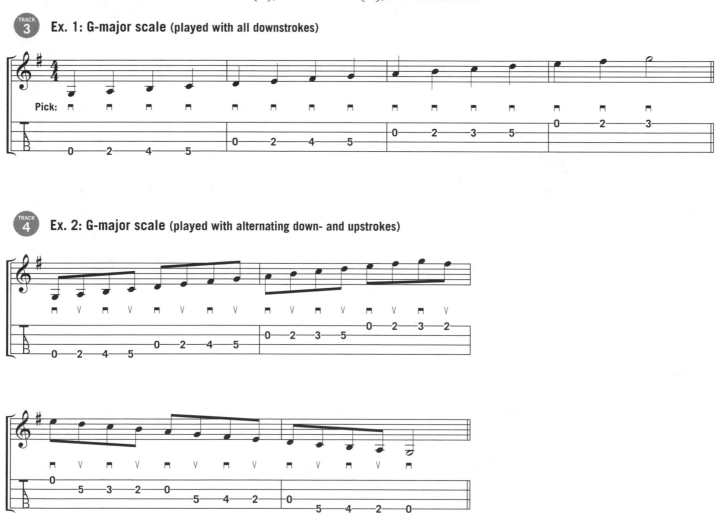

dominant seventh (F). In **Example 3,** add these three intervals to the G-major scale and practice with alternating down and up pick strokes, playing as slowly as necessary to maintain a steady tempo. Some players feel that practicing with a metronome is not "bluesy" . . . Playing with erratic time is less so.

To achieve a slurred third, you play the minor and major third (B♭ and B♮) together by sliding from one to the other using a single pick stroke or playing them in rapid succession using two strokes. In either case, fret both notes on the G string with your middle finger and those on the second string with your index finger.

The flatted fifth (D♭) is played on the G string at the sixth fret and on the A string at the fourth fret (in both cases with the ring finger), often in combination with the fifth—the open D string or the A string at the fifth fret. The flatted or dominant seventh (F) is played on the D string on the third fret with the middle finger, and on the E string at the first fret with the index finger.

Ex. 3: G-major scale with added blues notes

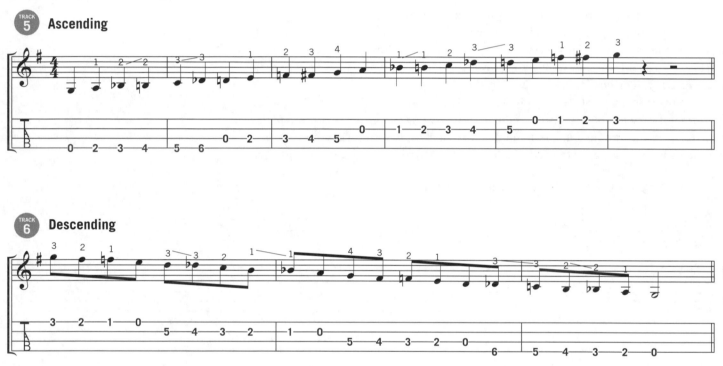

The scale pattern in Example 3 contains basic blues vocabulary in the key of G, first position. **Examples 4 and 5** are a couple of two-octave patterns that show a little about how they work. Example 4 incorporates all the notes in a G-major scale along with the blue notes in an "imitation" pattern; you alternate between adjacent higher and lower notes in the sequence. Example 5 uses only the tonic and fifth plus the blue notes, which produces a harder blues sound. Maintain the same fingering we've been using and practice with down- and upstrokes.

Ex. 4: Two-octave phrase with blue notes

TRACK 8 **Ex. 5: Phrase using only blue notes**

As you become familiar with these sounds and the fingering and pick techniques, try making up some phrases of your own or adding blue notes to melodies you already know. Listening to recordings and live performances of blues mandolin will also help you develop your ear.

TREMOLO

One more technique basic to mandolin playing in general and blues in particular is worth practicing from the start. Pick tremolo is the device used to create sustained tones on an instrument that otherwise produces notes with a relatively short decay rate. For tremolo, you play rapid down and up pick strokes. A quarter note, normally played with a single downstroke, can be divided into two eighth notes played with a down- and upstroke. Four alternating pick strokes in the same time value yield 16th notes, and eight pick strokes produce 32nd notes, which sound as a sustained tremolo that can be used on any note of a beat or more in duration. Tremolo with 32nd notes is particularly effective on half and whole note phrases. In the notation, tremolo is indicated with a pair of angled lines.

While developing the picking speed it takes to play smooth tremolo, remember to keep your hand and wrist relaxed. Practice with **Example 6,** a bluesy run using pick tremolo. As you can hear, I slide into some of these notes from a lower fret.

TRACK 9 **Ex. 6: Pick tremolo**

Songs in G

O nce your hands are comfortable in playing position and ears tuned to the blues, you're ready to start using the best method of all to improve your playing skills. Let's play some songs!

SHORT'NIN' BREAD

Hear how adding some slurred thirds and flatted fifths gives a bluesy sound, even to the familiar melody of this old folk song.

Use alternating down and up pick strokes throughout, except on the rhythm figure played on the G and D strings in bar 10, which is strummed with all downstrokes (and sounds a bit like rock 'n' roll!). As with much of the music included here, emphasize the second and fourth beats of each measure—the backbeats—to get a swinging feel.

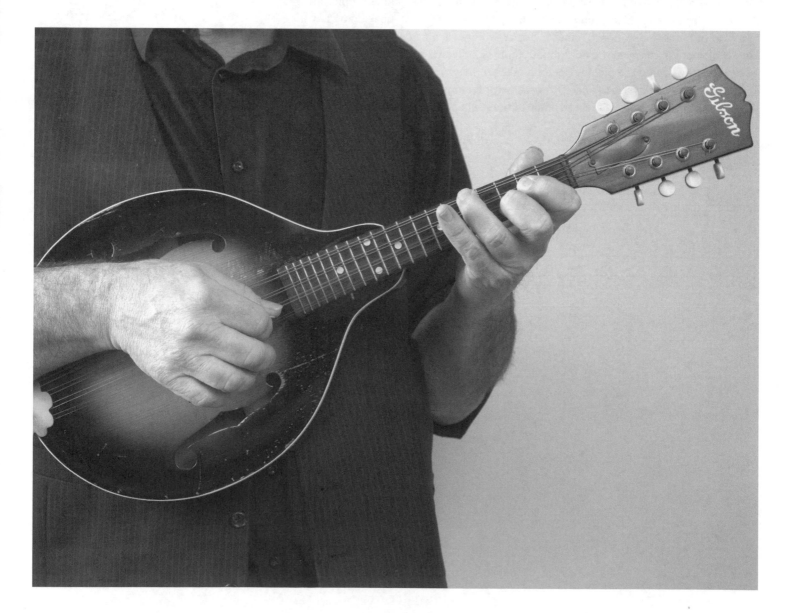

Short'nin' Bread

Traditional, arranged by Steve James

MANDOLIN BOOGIE

Did someone mention rock 'n' roll? "Mandolin Boogie" is a 12-bar riff constructed around standard blues chord changes. Use down and up pick strokes to swing the eighth-note pattern up to the quarter notes in the turnaround phrase in bar 11, which are played with downstrokes. The fingering will be familiar from the scale examples in the previous chapter; use your index, middle, and ring fingers (but don't curl that little one up!). All the blue notes are in there. Listen to how they work around the changes.

Despite its relatively high voice and bright sound, the mandolin can be a very effective rhythm instrument, as can be heard here. Polish this one up and bring it to a jam session, along with your blues licks in G, and see what the guitar and harmonica players do when you break it out.

Mandolin Boogie

Music by Steve James

 Played Slowly   **Played up to Tempo**

YOU DON'T KNOW MY MIND

This simple arrangement of an old country blues standard is based on a version learned from Howard Armstrong, who liked to play it onstage and pass it around when he led a workshop session. The fingering in the first position should be becoming familiar by now. If not, back up and practice your lickology from the "Blue Notes and Tremolo" chapter. Pick with all downstrokes, except for the tremolo on the whole notes in bars 3, 6, and 12. This effect can be added once you've learned the melody well enough to play it up to tempo. Howard used to tear through this one pretty quick when he got in the mood, but the song works at a slow or medium tempo as well. Don't play faster than you can count, and vice versa.

The G7 chord shape in bar 3 is fretted with the index finger on the A string, the middle finger on the D string, and the ring finger on the E. More chords coming up.

Note that in the slow version audio track, I simplify the part somewhat. For instance, in the opening measures I do not play the three-note chord indicated in the notation; I play only the G on the third fret of the E string.

You Don't Know My Mind

Traditional, arranged by Steve James

TRACK 15 Played Slowly   **TRACK 16** Played up to Speed

Changing Keys

Now for a 12-bar blues of a different kind, and in a different key! Although the next song is in the key of D, the fingering remains largely the same as what we played in the key of G. The slide from F to F♯ on the first string is played with the index finger, a slurred third at the first and second fret. Another blue third is played on the D string by sliding from fret three to four with the middle finger or fretting them separately using the middle and ring fingers. The ring finger covers notes at the fifth fret, just as it has in the tunes you've been playing in G. Just move everything over a string. It's that easy.

FLORIDA BLUES

The music of the violin is a good source for mandolin repertoire since the two instruments are tuned the same way. "Florida Blues" started out as a flag waver for early Grand Ole Opry fiddle star Arthur Smith and has been played at even faster tempos by bluegrass fiddlers like Chubby Wise.

Once again, take it easy with the tempo at first and you'll get more drive out of the tune. Use down- and upstrokes on the eighth-note passages and downstrokes to emphasize the longer notes. This version is based on one played for me by premier Bay Area bow dragger Suzy Thompson. It's a very bluesy tune, even though the only blue notes are the insistent slurred thirds. The two parts, as you'll hear, are nearly identical.

Florida Blues

Traditional, arranged by Steve James

TRACK **17** Part A, Played Slowly   TRACK **18** Part B, Played Slowly   TRACK **19** Played up to Tempo

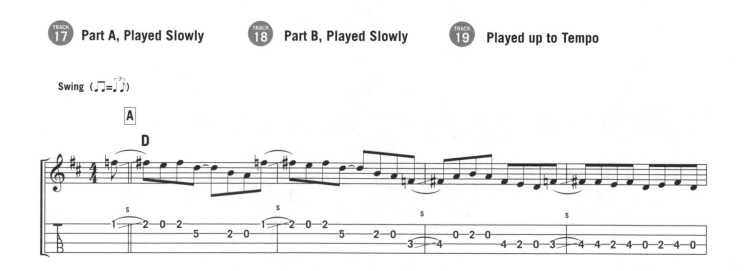

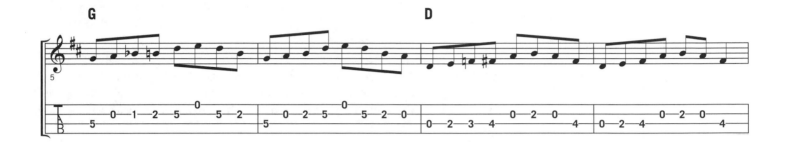

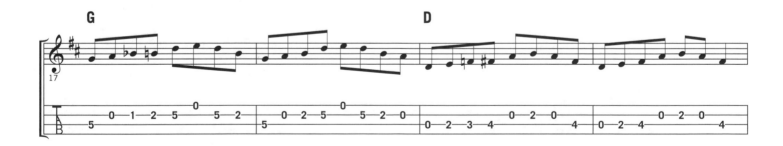

CLOSING AND TRANSPOSING

The pieces you've been playing up to this point have been in first position using open strings. Now it's time to put that fourth finger to work and "close up" the fretting pattern. The next melody, **"Slow Blues in D,"** should be familiar if you've heard songs like "Sitting On Top of the World" or "You Got to Move." Start by using downstrokes; when you can play the melody at a slow but steady tempo, play the second version, with tremolo on the longer notes as indicated below.

Up to this point you've been playing the E and A notes on the corresponding open strings; now you'll use your little finger to fret them on the A and D strings at the seventh fret. The exception is the A note in the sixth bar. Fret that with the ring finger on the D string after using the index to slide from C to C♯ on the A string, forming a partial A chord in second position.

Slow Blues in D

Music by Steve James

TRACK 20 **Played without Tremolo**   **TRACK 21** **Played with Tremolo**

When you can play the melody (and the descending turnaround phrase in bar 8) in D, you may want to try taking advantage of the closed position to explore two basic methods of key transposing on the mandolin. As you know from playing "Florida Blues" in D and comparing it to previous tunes in G, any phrase played on three strings or fewer can be transposed to another key by moving it over a string. Try the same thing in reverse with this arrangement. In **"Slow Blues in G,"** you use the same fingering as you did in D but start the melody on the second (A) string instead of the first. Now you are playing in the key of G with the tonic on the D string at the fifth fret.

Slow Blues in G

Music by Steve James

 Played up to Tempo

Another way to change keys is to move an entire closed fingering pattern up or down the fingerboard. For example, you can play this arrangement in the key of E by moving the fingering up the neck two frets and starting the melody line with a slide from the third to fourth frets on the E string (G to G♯, a slurred third) using the index finger—see **"Slow Blues in E."** The tonic E on the A string at the seventh fret is played with the ring finger, and the rest of the tune follows the same pattern used in D and G.

Slow Blues in E

Music by Steve James

 Played up to Tempo

Take this short lesson in transposing as far as you'd like at this point. It's a basic answer to a question that I've heard from many mandolinists since I first asked it myself: "What do I do when they're playing in E?" More song arrangements using closed position playing in different keys are included later in the book.

Accompaniment Made Easy

In addition to having a distinctive solo voice, the mandolin can be used to accompany other instruments and singers. Its bright tone and strong attack or "bark" make it ideal for chopping out rhythm chords. To start out, here are some effective, easy-to-play backup figures that make use of double stops.

A chord, by definition, is made up of at least three notes. On mandolin, with its double-string courses, a chord partial containing only two notes (a double stop) will often work in place of a full chord. **"Double-Stop Blues,"** a 12-bar blues progression with an ending turnaround, is played entirely on the G and D strings. Start by fretting the G string at the fourth fret with your middle finger and the D string at the fifth fret with your ring finger; these notes are B and G, which are two of the notes in a full G chord triad (G, B, D). By fretting the D string at the third fret (F) with your index finger while leaving the middle finger in place on the G string, you alter the voicing to a partial G7 chord. Similar two-string shapes are used to make C, C7, D, and D7 chord partials.

The progression ends with a four-beat turnaround in the 11th bar: G–G7–C–C7 before resolving on G. Play with pick downstrokes, and mute with your fretting hand after each stroke to get a swinging, "chonka-chonka" feel.

This arrangement can be used to accompany many 12-bar blues songs, including the one that follows.

Double-Stop Blues

Music by Steve James

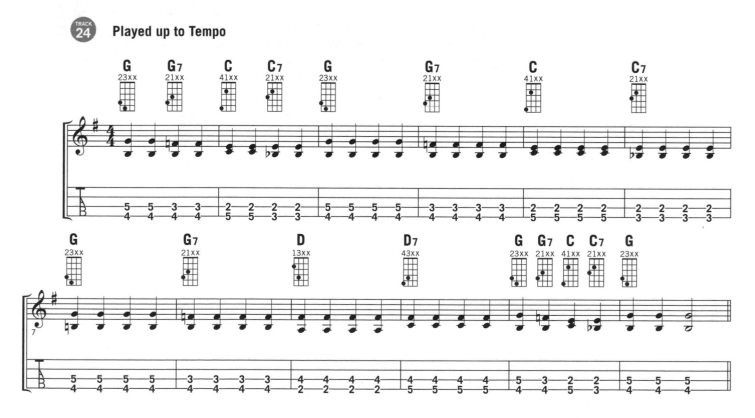

DUPREE BLUES

A number of popular songs ("Since I Met You, Baby," "The Wee Midnight Hours") have used the same melody as this blues ballad, first recorded in the 1920s. This mandolin arrangement uses double stops in the first and second position and fretted with the index and ring fingers, punctuated by some single-note fills. The turnaround (G–G7–C–C7) is the same as that in "Double-Stop Blues," but it's voiced on the D and A strings. The fills in bars 3 and 7, which ascend and descend in half step (one fret) intervals, and the second-position double stops played around the fifth to ninth frets in the first two bars, are versatile harmony devices. Again, this song was a favorite of Howard Armstrong's.

Forming Major and Seventh Chords

Following are a series of four-string chord shapes; included are major chord triads and related shapes that employ an added dominant seventh. Six of these shapes are formed with a combination of open and fretted strings in the first position. Four of them require the use of only two fingers (which, in part, explains the popularity of the mandolin).

The remaining eight chord shapes are closed; that is, they include no open strings and are therefore movable. For example, to form an F7 chord using the E7 shape, simply move it up the fingerboard one fret. This alters the tonic note (played on the third string and indicated by an asterisk below the diagram) and, consequently, the chord designation, from E to F.

Note that a major chord triad is formed by using the tonic, third, and fifth notes of the corresponding major scale. To alter a major chord to a seventh, simply add the dominant or flatted seventh degree of the same scale. The use of these chord shapes will be detailed further in the context of specific songs.

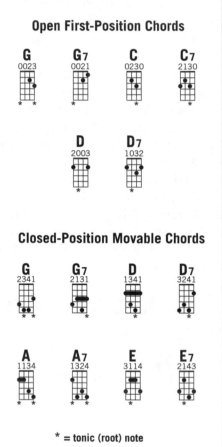

Open First-Position Chords

Closed-Position Movable Chords

* = tonic (root) note

Dupree Blues

Traditional, arranged by Steve James

 Played up to Tempo

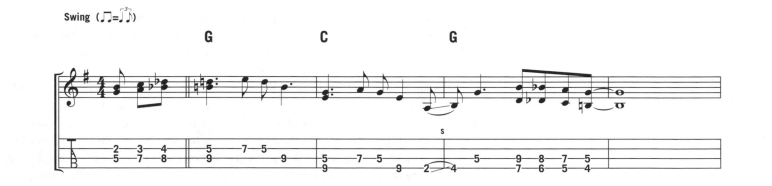

Moving to A

Get your mandolin on; here's a bit of a workout in a new key. For these two variations on a 12-bar blues in A the fingering is closed, and single-note runs are punctuated by a variety of double stops and strummed passages. They also make use of pick tremolo of up to a full measure in duration.

The unique harmonies in **"Blues in A"** include an interesting D7 double stop in bar 5 of the first part and a D-minor chord voicing in bar 18 of the second part. The F♯ that occurs repeatedly is sometimes played on the E string at the second fret; at other times it's played on the A string at the ninth fret, where it's stopped by the fourth finger. Use your index and ring fingers to fret the descending run in bar 10, from E on the A string. This requires a quick position change (but you'll recognize the lick from previous pieces in other keys). The deliberate tempo makes it easier to practice some of these fairly ambitious passages—worth the effort because this tune is full of useful phrases, and the key of A is a favorite with blues guitarists.

The elements of this arrangement are gleaned from an improvisational romp entitled "Prater Blues," recorded in 1928 by the remarkable mandolinist Matthew Prater with guitarist Nap Hayes.

Blues in A

Traditional, arranged by Steve James

 Part A   Part B

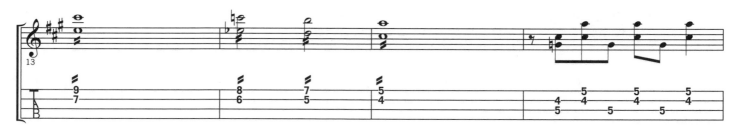

Melody and Accompaniment

The next four transcriptions pair up melody and accompaniment parts for some often-interpreted blues favorites.

CORRINA

The evergreen "Corrina" has been heard in every style from country blues and jug band to western swing. In this arrangement, the melody is played closed using double stops and tremolo. The pickup phrase at the beginning has the same series of double stops as "Dupree Blues"; they're just moved over a string to sound in C. Fret with the index, middle, and ring fingers and play with downstrokes, except for the tremolo phrases and the single-note tag at the end.

The double stops on the low strings that comprise the accompaniment are those introduced in "Double-Stop Blues" but played in the key of C. Move it on over. On the audio tracks you can hear the melody and accompaniment parts separately and then played together.

Corrina

Traditional, arranged by Steve James

TROUBLE IN MIND

The melody part as written here is not complicated—first position with a few double-stop harmonies and a little tremolo—but this old tune doesn't require much dressing up. The accompaniment, with some three- and four-string chord shapes we haven't used yet, is a different type of blues progression from those preceding. Play over the melody first; then work on fingering the chords as diagrammed below and played on the audio until you can play them in sequence.

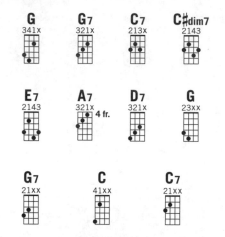

The diminished chord in bar 4 is a handy shape, like a C7 chord with the tonic C raised to C♯. Spelled A♯, E, C♯, G, this chord contains all the intervals of the four-note diminished scale and inverts every three frets: Move the shape from the second to fourth frets, as diagrammed, to the fifth to seventh frets, and it comes out C♯, G, E, A♯ . . . the same four notes in a different order.

The last four bars of the accompaniment are a set of rhythm changes, G–E7–A7–D7, followed by a standard turnaround. The A7 and D7 are played by forming the same chord shape around consecutive frets: fourth to sixth and third to fifth, respectively. The same shape can be used around frets five through seven for an alternate E7 voicing. It's really just a double stop with a third and two sevenths, but the extra note fattens the sound up a bit. Play the sequence with downstrokes and an emphasis on the backbeats.

Trouble in Mind

Traditional, arranged by Steve James

CARELESS LOVE

This 16-bar song was part of the earliest blues repertoire and has antecedents in American and European folk song; that is to say, it's old. Here the melody is played mostly with double stops on low and high string pairs in closed positions, but the arrangement includes a single-string tag in which the E♭ on the A string at the sixth fret is played against the open E string. This manner of playing a slurred third is commonly used by blues mandolinists. The accompaniment, like that of "Trouble in Mind," contains three- and four-string seventh and diminished chords.

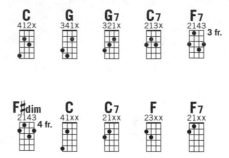

The F7 chord has the same fingering as the E7 used in "Trouble in Mind" moved up a fret. Alter it to an F♯dim by raising the tonic note on the D string one fret, a half step, from F to F♯. Limitations of space preclude much discourse about diminished scales and chords but, in case you're wondering at this point: yes, a diminished chord can be named for any of its four intervals depending on how it's used.

Careless Love

Traditional, arranged by Steve James

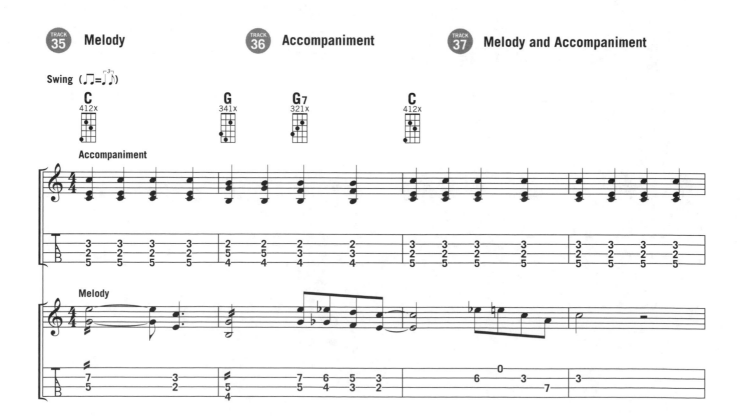

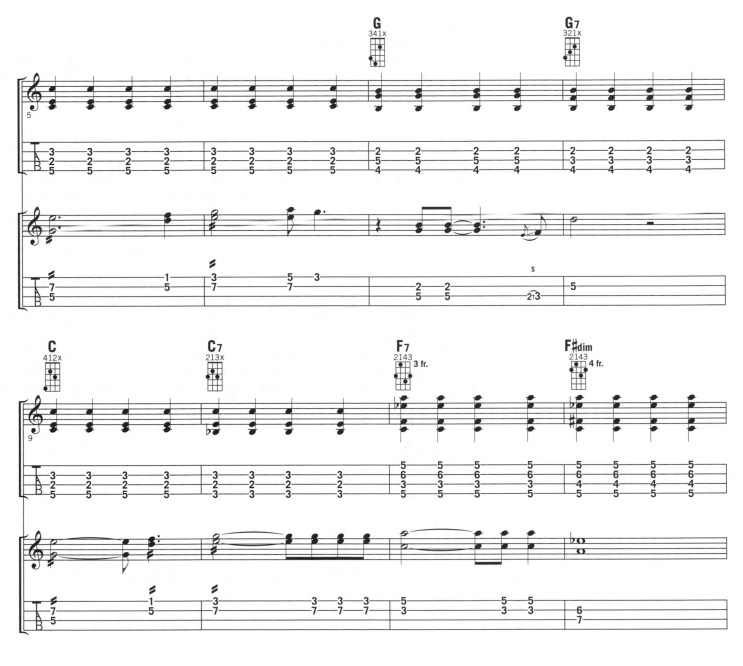

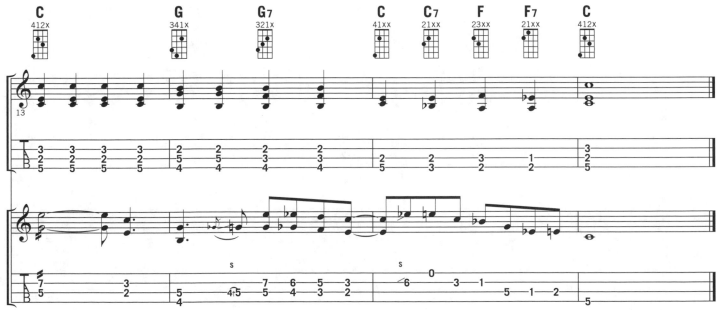

GAMBLER'S BLUES

Last in this set of four themes with accompaniment arrangements is another blues icon. Unlike any other piece in this book, "Gambler's Blues" is in a minor key. Two versions of the melody are transcribed. They are alike except for being an octave apart. There are also two accompaniment parts with low and high inversions of the three chords, Am, E7, and F7.

The fingering on all four parts is closed except for a single open string in the high melody. For the low part, stop the A and E notes at the second fret with your index finger, sliding into the E from E♭, the flatted fifth, one fret below. Use your ring finger at the fifth fret and middle finger on the third and fourth. The D and A at the seventh fret are played with the fourth finger. The high melody is fretted with the index, middle, and ring fingers.

When sliding from E♭ to E on the A string, let your pick downstroke sound the open E string as well; this is another example of contrasting one string played at the sixth fret with the open string above it. Both melody parts are played mostly with pick downstrokes; add tremolo to sustain the notes in bars 3 and 11. The Am chord in the low accompaniment part is fretted with the index and middle fingers, while the E7 and F7 chord shapes are familiar from previous songs. The three-string chords in the high part are played with the index, middle, and ring fingers; in all of them the middle finger frets the G string.

Note that in a minor key, the flatted fifth and dominant seventh are the same intervals as in the corresponding major key. A minor third is one fret (half step) below a major third, and a slurred minor third is effected by playing it in combination with the second degree of the scale, a half step below it.

Gambler's Blues

Traditional, arranged by Steve James

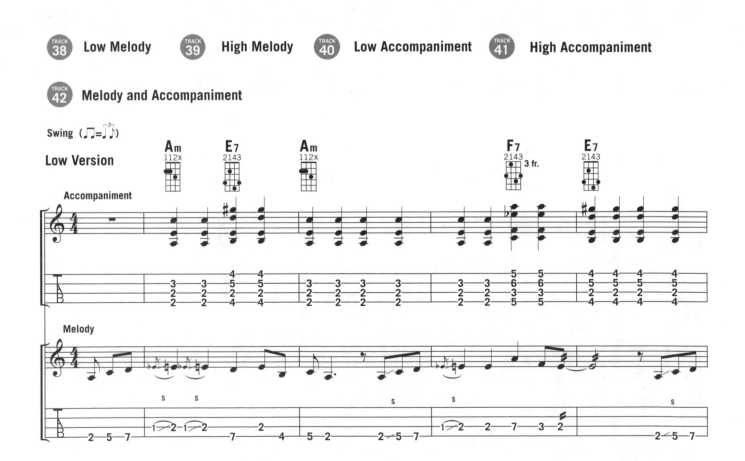

High Version

Gibson F-2, circa 1917.

OPEN TUNING AND SLIDE MANDOLIN

"Who said both strings in a pair have to be the same note?" The question was posed by mandolinist Matt Circely one late night in Port Townsend, Washington, where we had been sitting under the stars with our instruments since . . . earlier. The question was in response to my posit that slide mandolin, except as a stage gag or party trick, wasn't possible because four strings wasn't enough for a viable open tuning. We were twisting tuners in an instant, and wound up with this: gG Dg Bd dd.

The low G strings are tuned in an octave rather than in unison. One D string remains at pitch, the other raised to G. One A string is raised a whole step to B; the other raised five half steps to D. The highest course is lowered a whole step so both strings sound in unison as a D. Playing across all four courses sounds strange, but it is a G triad (G, B, D) with doubled tonic and fifth, as with open-G tuning on guitar, and it works!

Matt and I didn't break any strings that night, but that was just luck; and tuning strings that far above their intended pitch is bad for the instrument. I picked a designated slide mandolin and swapped strings around until my G course had an A string for the high note, and I subbed another A string for the G in the D course. One of the strings in the A course was replaced with an E string. The E strings remained the same. The gauges ran like this:

.016/.038w   .026w/.016   .016/.011   .011/.011

Although I fingerpick when playing slide guitar, a flatpick suits me better for slide mandolin. Of course, there isn't a "standard' or traditional method; there aren't enough players to establish one . . . yet. I use the slide in the same way as for guitar, wearing it on my fourth finger and muting behind it with the flat of my index. Playing in tune on such a short scale requires some attention, but it can be done. (I've recorded a slide mandolin/guitar duet that required no digital pitch correction.) You'll find that this tuning has some sweet spots, along with a few that aren't. The first thing I tried was the Delta anthem "Roll and Tumble," and a verse of it, along with an intro phrase, is what's shown here.

Slide Mandolin

Music by Steve James

 Tune-up: g G, D g, B d, d d

 Played up to Tempo

Intro

Freely

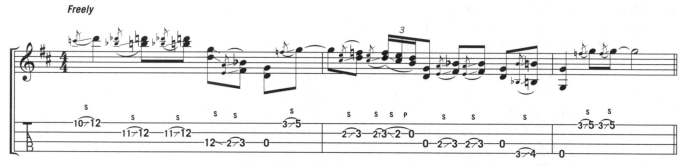

Verse

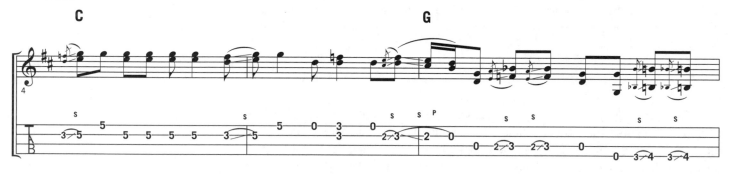

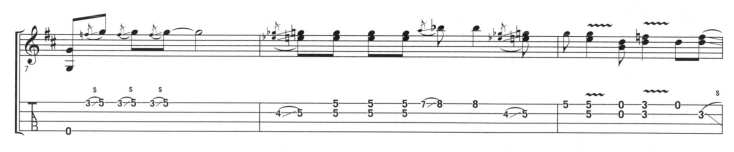

RECOMMENDED RESOURCES

RECORDING

Various artists, *Rags, Breakdowns, Stomps, and Blues: Vintage Mandolin Music 1927–1946*, Document 32-20-3 (document-records.com). This anthology is the "desert island disc" for blues mandolin, with prewar tracks from Howard Armstrong, Coley Jones, Charley McCoy, Matthew Prater, Yank Rachell, Vol Stevens, and more.

BOOK

Rich Del Grosso, *Mandolin Blues from Memphis to Maxwell Street*, Hal Leonard (halleonard. com). A detailed and dedicated study of the styles and repertoire of the early blues mandolin masters, this volume includes transcriptions of pieces by Armstrong, Rachell, McCoy, and many others.

DVD

Steve James, *Learn to Play Blues Mandolin*, Homespun Tapes (homespun.com). In this two-part video lesson, the author, accompanied by John Sebastian (disc one) and Del Rey (disc two), demonstrates a variety of blues mandolin techniques and songs.

FILM

Louie Bluie, directed by Terry Zwigoff (1985). This documentary on the life and music of Howard Armstrong includes performances by Ted Bogan, Yank Rachell, and "Banjo" Ikey Robinson.

WEB

Mandolin Café, mandolincafe.com. The definitive mandolin website offers lessons, articles, a forum, classifieds, reviews, and a marketplace page, plus links to recordings and resources of interest to mandolinists in any style.

ABOUT THE AUTHOR

Photo by Lucy Piper

Steve James found his first mandolin, a play-worn plywood Strad-O-Lin with painted-on binding, in a Tennessee pawnshop. By the next day he had taught himself to play the blues in G. Some years and several key changes later, Steve keeps his Austin address and a second home on the road, playing live shows and teaching at music workshop programs. He has recorded several albums of original roots music featuring his guitar, slide guitar, mandolin, and singing; played sessions for numerous other artists; and made instructional DVDs on guitar and mandolin for Homespun. In addition, he's been writing articles, lessons, and books for *Acoustic Guitar* since issue number one. See and hear more at Steve's website, stevejames.com.

NEVER MISS A BEAT

Subscribe to Acoustic Guitar

Get the #1 resource for all things acoustic guitar delivered right to your door.

EVERY ISSUE INCLUDES

- Tips on technique
- Essential gear reviews
- Sheet music for the songs you want to learn
- Interviews with your favorite players
- Lessons to help you become a better acoustic guitar player
- And more

Be the acoustic guitarist you want to be with the magazine for acoustic guitar players, by acoustic guitar players.

Sign up today!

GUITAR LEARNING HAS GONE MOBILE

Acoustic Guitar U—The Next Level in Guitar Learning

No music book? No music stand? No sheet music? NO PROBLEM.

Log onto **AcousticGuitarU.com** from your PC, laptop, tablet, or smartphone and check out our ever-growing library of online guitar lessons, complete courses, and songs to learn. Enjoy:

- **Best-of-the-web audio and video instruction in a wide variety of styles and topics**

- **Easy-to-follow lessons for all levels from total beginner to advanced**

- **Streaming content, which means no more time spent waiting for files to download**

Learn acoustic guitar anytime, anywhere. All you need is access to the Internet.

MORE TITLES FROM STRINGLETTER

BOOKS

Learn authentic techniques, hone your skills, and expand your understanding of musical essentials with the help of our song and lesson books including:

Explore Alternate Tunings

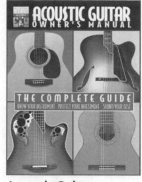

Acoustic Guitar Owner's Manual

Acoustic Blues Guitar Essentials

Classical Guitar Answer Book

The Acoustic Guitar Method Complete Edition

Songwriting and the Guitar

GUIDES

Become a better guitarist and more informed instrument owner with our range of informative guides. Acoustic Guitar Guides offer video and written instruction and can be downloaded as individual lessons, or complete courses. Popular titles include:

Acoustic Guitar Amplification Essentials: Complete Edition
Get answers to all your acoustic amplification questions with this complete guide series featuring both video and written instruction. Learn how to use monitors, PAs, EQ, and effects; discover the differences between the various pickups and how to install them, and learn how to choose and position microphones to capture your guitar's natural tone.
By Doug Young.

Acoustic Guitar Slide Basics: Complete Edition
Master one of the great styles of American roots music with the help of these nine progressive lessons (video and written instruction) on the fundamentals of acoustic slide guitar.
By David Hamburger.

Acoustic Blues Guitar Basics: Fingerstyle Blues
Learn basic fingerpicking blues patterns played by blues greats like Reverend Gary Davis and Robert Johnson. Try Piedmont and Delta fingerpicking styles, and play two complete 12-bar fingerstyle tunes.
By Orville Johnson.

Visit **Store.AcousticGuitar.com** today for the full range of Acoustic Guitar products.